SUNDAY EXPRESS & DAILY EXPRESS
CARTOONS

Thirty-eighth Series

AN EXPRESS BOOKS PUBLICATION

Printed in Great Britain by Purnell and Sons (Book Production) Ltd., Paulton, Bristol

£1.75

FOREWORD

by

Sir ALASTAIR BURNET

Britain's Top

TV Commentator

Gilesland is, as everyone knows, a country wholly surrounded by choppy seas and duffers in boats. Its pastures are peopled by idle cattle, idle farmhands and even idler earls. No snow falls there that does not end up impacting on the necks of vicars and postmen. No rain falls except to raise the grass for the lawn-mower industry.

It is not a democracy but an anarchy, the urban guerrillas led by a gerontic passionara in black. Its pubs never close, its butlers never falter. Its men are pitiable but persevering, its women patient in their superiority, its children numerous. It is full of mischief. We have to shout on News at Ten to make ourselves heard above the Gilesland hubbub. Its books are more often thrown than read. Mostly English is spoken.

We have all lived there for many years, and our memories of each year are full of grace. Long may it flourish, and its begetter thrive!

"I hope the Prime Minister makes a better job of her carving than your father."
(The Prime Minister promised drastic cuts)

Sunday Express, June 12th, 1983

"He's more scared of losing his head now he's won than he was of losing his seat before the election."

Daily Express, June 14th, 1983

"Next time you clean-bowl the Colonel, it's 'Howzat, Sir?' not 'Gotcha Blimpo!' "

Daily Express, June 16th, 1983

"Remember the days when all the males in this house had a fortnight's moan if we switched Wimbledon on?"

Sunday Express, June 19th, 1983

"Permission to remove tomahawk from birthday present, Ma'am? HRH has already scalped the butler,
the first footman, the second cook . . ."

Daily Express, June 21st, 1983

"Blame TV sex for him asking you for a date—and Minder for the thump on the nose when you turned him down."

Daily Express, June 23rd, 1983

"I am not prepared to sit all afternoon discussing the merits of bringing back hanging for umpires and linesmen, Mr. McEnroe."

Sunday Express, June 26th, 1983

"We hear you've been trying to flog your story for blood money of
'How I booked Chief Constable Gregory for parking one Sunday in '77' "

Daily Express, June 28th, 1983

"I get it all the time — 'Look at the speed of Ginny Wade and Billie Jean King and they are twice your age . . .' "

Daily Express, June 30th, 1983

"No I don't look at it this way — I don't think it's not only saving petrol it's doing me good."

Sunday Express, July 3rd, 1983

"It was bad enough getting him dressed when he worked in the Commons."

Daily Express, July 5th, 1983

"No, Mr. Murphy—I do not think your idea is the cure for the Church being 'dull',
'old-fashioned' and 'uninspiring' as the Bible Society survey puts it."

Sunday Express, July 10th, 1983

"Let's see if we can find daddy a category that qualifies him for hanging."

Daily Express, July 12th, 1983

"There must be a clause in her contract that governs the wearing apparel of Mrs Jones during office hours."

Daily Express, July 14th, 1983

"At least you haven't got a grandma who keeps telling you this heatwave
is nothing compared with the Punjab in 1908."

Sunday Express, July 17th, 1983

"I'm not knocking his new gear—I simply said I wonder how he'd rate with the top tailors' survey."

Daily Express, July 19th, 1983

"When it comes to entertainment, the visitors are not exactly Tommy Coopers."

Daily Express, July 21st, 1983

"Dad! The ferry strike's over—we can go to Zeebrugge for the weekend after all."

Sunday Express, July 24th, 1983

"I've locked up the fridge, cut off the power, called in police protection, next door are looking after the cat—
I think it's safe to pop down to the shops."

Daily Express, July 26th, 1983

"We could be in Greece, or Sri Lanka, or worse still—Reggie could have had that damn boat finished
in time for Cowes week."

Sunday Express, July 31st, 1983

"You're still liable for prosecution, sir, the ban has not been officially lifted yet."

Daily Express, August 2nd, 1983

"You know what their defence will be—'Capt. Mark Phillips lets them jump over Land Rovers at his house'."

Sunday Express, August 7th, 1983

"Morning Michelangelo. As the Arts Council have lavished £50,000 on your Work of Art, you shouldn't have any trouble paying the fine for depositing litter on the pavement."

Daily Express, August 9th, 1983

"Poor Louis, his new creation has the bricks, the tyres, AND a baked bean tin, but they've only sent him a £60,000 grant."

Sunday Express, August 14th, 1983

"Well, well! You've been worrying about moles at the office the whole damn holiday . . .!"

Daily Express, August 18th, 1983

"We'll give them five more minutes to notice us or it will be on cardigans."

Sunday Express, August 21st, 1983

"Of course it's not a very good snap of you, Grandma—that's a snap of the old harbour buoy
on the end of the pier."

Daily Express, August 25th, 1983

"Never mind surveys proving children don't like British holidays—at 80p a go kindly look as if you do."

Sunday Express, August 28th, 1983

"You're lucky, you can have a nice easy day to get over the holiday."

Daily Express, August 30th, 1983

"When I said if it was wet on Saturday they could use the Church Hall I didn't mean thro' Sunday."

Sunday Express, September 4th, 1983

"Most of them start: 'Went to the seaside, smashing punch-up with the Old Bill'."

Daily Express, September 6th, 1983

"Flinging her £1 million about before she's won it—new hat!"

Daily Express, September 8th, 1983

"David Steel's wife thinks it's bad for the family when he's away from home—I think it's extremely bad for me when I'm not."

Daily Express, September 13th, 1983

"Right! Before the service—all new miniature televisions up sleeves on table!"

Sunday Express, September 18th, 1983

"Carry on, you were saying how you would have handled the British boat in the America's Cup."

Sunday Express, September 25th, 1983

"Talking of Sportsmanship and Sabotage, Rodney — I haven't forgotten the time you got me plastered the night before the Round the Island race."

Daily Express, September 27th, 1983

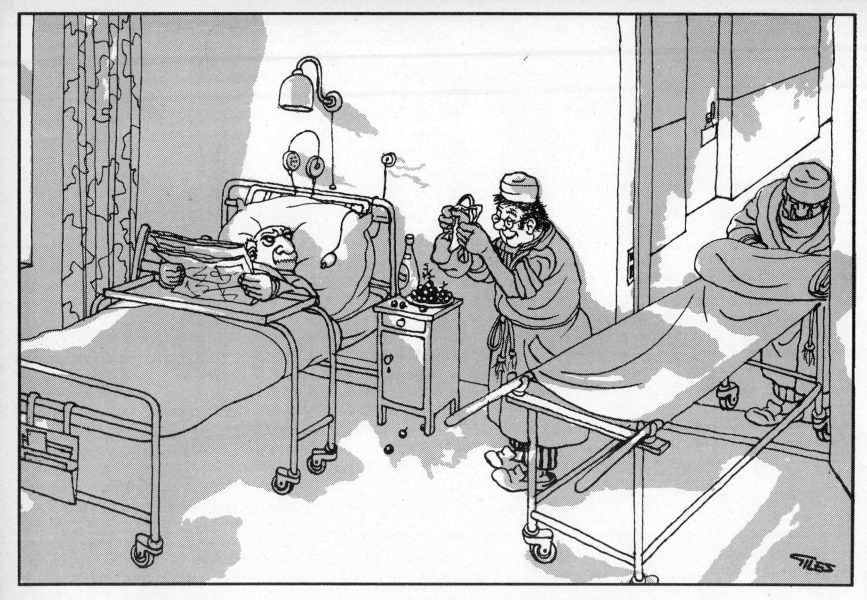

"Up we get! Owing to staff cuts, me and Harry are whipping your old duodenal out this morning."

Daily Express, September 29th, 1983

"I was only joking—I said: 'Wakey, wakey, Sir, you've just been elected leader of the Labour Party'."

Sunday Express, October 2nd, 1983

"Cut! Here cometh the law."

Sunday Express, October 9th, 1983

"I don't worry too much about my Jim. He never gets over-excited without a gun at his head."

Daily Express, October 11th, 1983

"Charlie, find out if it even touched my new Rolls and if it did, send it back!"

Daily Express, October 13th, 1983

"Moral obligations being all the rage—I suggest you teach that Airedale thing of yours a few."

Sunday Express, October 16th, 1983

"Did you read about that customer who left a waitress £162,000?"

Sunday Express, October 23rd, 1983

"Mum, Grandma's won a Daily Express racehorse."

Daily Express, October 25th, 1983

"Mrs. Thatcher did have a word with the President about the inadvisability of parking it on your allotment but I guess the President told us to still go ahead."

Daily Express, October 27th, 1983

"One thing about living on a less exotic isle than Grenada, you're not likely to get troops dropping in on you without notice."

Sunday Express, October 30th, 1983

"His boy put it on his head at a Halloween party and he can't get it off."

Daily Express, November 1st, 1983

"Butch must learn that the law that says it's all right for nude dancers to bite policemen, doesn't apply to grumpy Airedales."

("Nude bites policeman . . ." remarkable headline, yesterday's paper)

Sunday Express, November 6th, 1983

"Everyone agrees with Egon Ronay's report on their appalling service, but some people keep quiet about it!"

Daily Express, November 8th, 1983

"MISS WORLD" LOGICAL THINKING COMPUTER TEST

GILES

"Look at it another way—as the computer brain test result has wiped that inane smile off your face you might win."

Daily Express, November 10th, 1983

"That's the kind of video nasty I'd ban from the home—two reels of Grandma and Vera paddling in Benidorm."

Sunday Express, November 13th, 1983

"Reckon we've got a late entry for the Miss World contest tonight—that's the fourth time she's washed her hair this week."

Daily Express, November 17th, 1983

"I think they're fascinated with your new image since they read you're all drunken racist bullies."

Sunday Express, November 20th, 1983

"ACHTUNG! Now you've all seen the pictures of the Queen walking in her sedan chair . . ."

Daily Express, November 22nd, 1983

"And Rajah—be a good chap and control those long rumbling tummy noises during the Commonwealth speeches."

Daily Express, November 24th, 1983

"Greenham and NGA pickets are enough for one week without bloody Cabbage Patch dolls."

Daily Express, December 1st, 1983

"Daddy got six stitches in his head queueing to get you one — at least come down and say 'hello'."

Sunday Express, December 4th, 1983

"He says if he'd been Joseph he'd have retaliated with a couple of Cruise missiles and blown Herod to kingdom come."

Daily Express, December 6th, 1983

"I'm getting a bit fed up with you climbing up here just to get your picture in the papers."

Sunday Express, December 11th, 1983

"Now your Christmas computerised exterminator has blown the TV set, can you make it find the matches
so we can mend the fuses?"

Daily Express, December 13th, 1983

"He must have heard about that dog who was awarded costs for biting a man—
Horatio has never bitten a Father Christmas before."

Daily Express, December 15th, 1983

"Grandma's been a great help. She's packed all the presents but forgot to label them which one's which."

Sunday Express, December 18th, 1983

"Miss won't come to any harm over Christmas—we've locked her in the cupboard."

Daily Express, December 20th, 1983

"But Charles—you were laughing when that girl threw a custard pie at you!"

Daily Express, December 22nd, 1983

"I don't know who he is—he called and said 'I'm Father Christmas' and he's been here all afternoon."

Daily Express, December 24th, 1983

"You know damn well the papers are out again today!"

Daily Express, December 27th, 1983

"We don't mind Grandma sharing our bedroom while we've got guests, but her embrocation and Evergreen ointment are the aggravation."

Daily Express, December 29th, 1983

"Never mind about Big Brother—Big Sister has been watching you . . . illegally parking since 8 o'clock."

Daily Express, January 3rd, 1984

"They gave Fred an alarm clock to wake him up to let him know he's arrived."

(For better timekeeping, BR presented free watches to staff)

Sunday Express, January 8th, 1984

"Tell Capt. Hornblower if he buys one, he'll be doing the washing up."

Daily Express, January 10th, 1984

"No, he wasn't chasing the Royals at ski-ing—he slipped base over head down the hospital steps photographing the Parkinson babe."

Daily Express, January 12th, 1984

"First the good news—President Mitterrand has apologised for the hijacking of your lorry, then the bad news—we've got it back."

Sunday Express, January 15th, 1984

"Not bad, but not quite up to the standard of Torvill and Dean."

Daily Express, January 17th, 1984

"A French doctor says 50 is a dangerous age to have a mistress. 'Ear that Rudolph Valentino?"

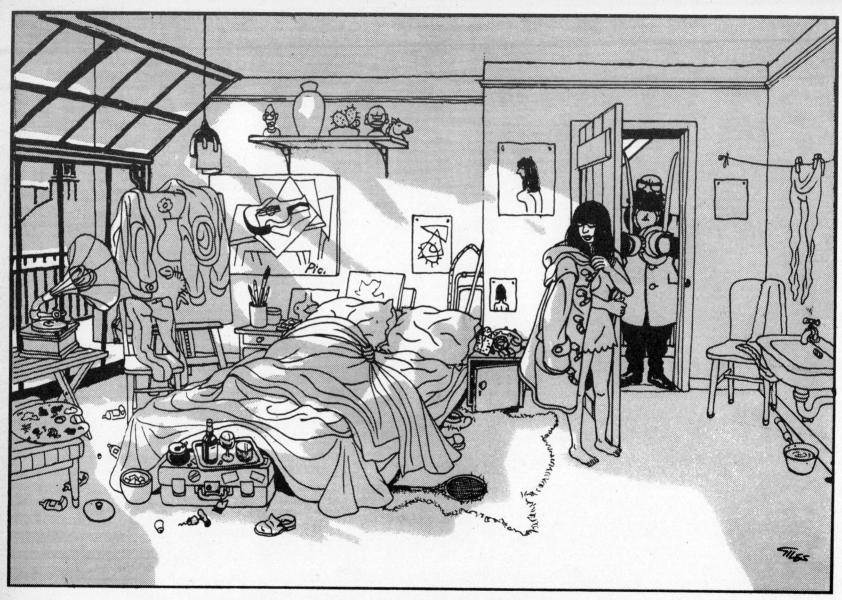

"You remember arguing in the pub about Mr. Heath, Mrs. Thatcher
and the Common Market, and challenging a French gentleman to a duel?"

Sunday Express, January 22nd, 1984

"I appreciate the Marriage Guidance Council's warning, but at two degrees below zero the dangers of making love in the back of a car do not exist."

Daily Express, January 24th, 1984

"In Chalkie's class the nearest we'd get to a saucy weekend in Paris would be a saucy weekend in Siberia."

(Schoolteachers were accused of 'dirty weekends' on the rates)

Daily Express, January 26th, 1984

"The ghost the Vicar is exorcising is learning some very naughty words."

(Princess Michael invited the church to exorcise a ghost)

Sunday Express, January 29th, 1984

"She's still in an uncontrollable rage over the babbling BBC commentators for ruining her snooker tournament."

Daily Express, January 31st, 1984

"It's YOU who ought to be up in front of the Jockey Club!"

Daily Express, February 2nd, 1984

"Two items off the agenda this morning — Cheltenham and the state of the pitch in New Zealand."

Daily Express, February 7th, 1984

"Dad, can you spare a minute—Ernie's raffled the house and a man's called to say he's won it."

(Headline: "Mansion raffled to make ends meet")

Sunday Express, February 12th, 1984

"Diana—where did you put William's old pram?"

Daily Express, February 14th, 1984

"How did that bit in the Bible go—'Beware of false prophets for they shall make money in my name'?"

Daily Express, February 16th, 1984

"I see your loved one is off to have a word with that goat who's been paying regular visits around here."

Sunday Express, February 19th, 1984

"You have been stuck behind me for three days? But I am not in the blockade—I live here!"

Daily Express, February 21st, 1984

"Soldiers of the Queen, Mrs Rabett—mounting the guard to keep the Press away."

Daily Express, February 23rd, 1984

"I'll give him just a couple of days of this: 'Madame Francoise didn't cook it like this in Lyons during the Great Blockade'."

Sunday Express, February 26th, 1984

"I have a dream! I dream that Victoria Principal walks in here and proposes to our candidate!"

Daily Express, February 28th, 1984

"Welcome back, Dawn Chorus — the oppressive silence was killing me!"

Daily Express, March 1st, 1984

"Mummy thought the French policeman who belted you was ever so good looking."

Sunday Express, March 4th, 1984

"A plague on redundant army chefs taking civilian jobs!"

Daily Express, March 6th, 1984

"Your wish to withdraw your account because of the Thatcher bank leak causes us great concern, especially as I see you are £3.50 in the red."

Daily Express, March 8th, 1984

"All we need to make him really happy is to find W. G. Grace was on pep pills."

Sunday Express, March 11th, 1984

"You were saying about the new tax on fish and chips being aimed only at the workers . . ."

Daily Express, March 15th, 1984

"I wouldn't bank on M'Lud letting you off because you are unemployed—it happened to be his pad which you did up."

Sunday Express, March 18th, 1984

"By the way, while you were away keeping order at the pits, someone nicked all our coal."

Daily Express, March 20th, 1984

"You are the 300th man whose grandmother's funeral is in Ottawa the same day as Torvill and Dean are there."

Daily Express, March 22nd, 1984

"Now the clocks have gone forward, Dad will have the nice light evenings to work on the garden."

Sunday Express, March 25th, 1984

"Peace be with you, Ma'am, they're some of ours. Mixture of King Hussein's bodyguard and S.A.S."

Daily Express, March 27th, 1984

"WE didn't say women jockeys should be banned from the National—it was Bob Champion who said they should be banned altogether."

Daily Express, March 29th, 1984

"There goes the Mother's Day cake we baked for Grandma."

Sunday Express, April 1st, 1984

"You won't let Dad take you to school dressed like that? Last night you were arguing that Boy George was the norm!"

Daily Express, April 3rd, 1984

"I remember writing in his report: 'Astute business sense, should do well'."

Daily Express, April 5th, 1984

"I can't bear people who address me as 'Luv'—especially when they follow it up with a crack across the head!"

Daily Express, April 10th, 1984

"Did you see Princess Anne smacked Master Phillips on his botwot at Badminton for being a naughty boy?"

Sunday Express, April 15th, 1984

"It's not official yet—just a practice run."

Daily Express, April 17th, 1984

"And send the bill to His Royal Majesty, Prince Andrew, U.K."

Daily Express, April 19th, 1984

"I know she's not likely to carry many £50 notes—but with her we check the pounds."

Daily Express, April 24th, 1984

"All these long sunny walks dad's taking us on—we'll get ever so brown."

Daily Express, April 26th, 1984

"Don't forget you're picking up Auntie Pauline and Uncle Jim for lunch."

Sunday Express, April 29th, 1984

"Here comes our instant strike-breaker."

Daily Express, May 1st, 1984

"She let us give her a lift to her polling booth providing we dropped her off at her sister's on the way home."

Sunday Express, May 6th, 1984

"I'm fed up with his same joke after every Bank Holiday: 'My! How you've all grown since I last saw you'."

Daily Express, May 8th, 1984

"If they all withdrew I'd look on it as a step towards world peace."

Daily Express, May 10th, 1984

"Hurry up, Mr Marathon—the other 20,141 left twenty minutes ago."

Sunday Express, May 13th, 1984

"Like last year, Butch, forget walkies for a few days after his marathon."

Daily Express, May 15th, 1984

"My Charlie gave me a new set of plugs for his bike for my birthday."

Daily Express, May 22nd, 1984

"Nice to read there are two people who like it so much they want to stay."

Daily Express, May 24th, 1984

"We said come and spend the holiday on the boat—we didn't say anything about being afloat."

Sunday Express, May 27th, 1984

"By the way, your daily help phoned—could she bring her four children as there is no school?"

Daily Express, May 29th, 1984

"There it is—June 6, 1944. You bet me £5 this was the war to end all wars. I bet you it wasn't. You owe me £5."

Daily Express, June 5th, 1984

"Bonjour, Monsieur — have you been here since yesterday's anniversary, or June 6, 1944?"

Daily Express, June 7th, 1984

"Well, you don't look like you've spent the week celebrating a war to make the world fit for heroes to live in."

Sunday Express, June 10th, 1984

"Rufus! Farmer says sorry to interrupt your day off he gave you to go to the EEC Elections, but he wants the key to the toolshed."

Daily Express, June 14th, 1984